W9-AJP-854

J
795.4
REI
Reisberg, Ken
Card tricks

DATE DUE			
DE 2 2 '92	AUG 0 3 '95	JY 1 8 '09	
FE 1 8 '93	JL 3 1 '96	FE 0 4 '16	
MR 4 '93	JUN 1 6 '97		
AP 1 '93	JL 0 3 '97		
	JUL 2 3 '97		
MY 2 2 '93	JUN 0 1 '98		
JY 2 9 '93	DEC 28 '98		
SE 1 3 '93	AG 0 2 '99		
OC 6 '93	SE 2 2 '00		
DEC 0 3 '94	MY 1 5 '03		
JUN 1 6 '95	MR 3 0 '05		
JUL 1 7 '95	JY 1 7 '09		

201-9500   PRINTED IN U.S.A.

EAU CLAIRE DISTRICT LIBRARY

an easy-read ACTIVITY book

CARD TRICKS
by Ken Reisberg
illustrated by
Arline and Marvin Oberman

A GROLIER COMPANY

Franklin Watts
New York/London/Toronto/Sydney
1980

EAU CLAIRE DISTRICT LIBRARY

81123

9/81 Watts 8.90

**For Harry,
The King of Card Tricksters**

R.L. 2.3 Spache Revised Formula

Library of Congress Cataloging in Publication Data

Reisberg, Ken.
  Card tricks.

  (An Easy-read activity book)
  SUMMARY: Instructions for doing mysterious card
tricks to entertain family and friends.
  1. Card tricks — Juvenile literature. [1. Card tricks]
I. Oberman, Marvin. II. Oberman, Arline. III. Title.
GV1549.R43   795.4'38   80-11111
ISBN 0-531-04137-9

Text copyright © 1980 by Ken Reisberg
Illustrations copyright © 1980 by
Arline and Marvin Oberman
All rights reserved
Printed in the United States of America
6 5 4 3 2 1

CONTENTS

Try all the card tricks in this book. There are many kinds of tricks to test your skill. Look them over and do them again and again. When you know how to do the tricks well, you can put on a card trick show for your family and friends.

When you are sure of yourself, the tricks will seem even more exciting and secret. Use your imagination! Make up things to say and do! Then try to make up your own card tricks.

RED AND BLACK

How to Do It

1. Shuffle the cards. Count out 26 cards one at a time on the table. Give these cards to a friend. Keep the other 26 cards for yourself.

2. Tell your friend that the number of red cards you have given him or her is exactly the same as the number of black cards you yourself have.

3. Count your black cards while your friend counts the red cards. Did the trick work?

♠ **1** This is one of the easiest card tricks. You only have to make sure to count out *exactly* 26 cards.

ONE WAY TO SHUFFLE CARDS

Put the cards on a table. Now take about half the cards from the top of the pack. Put them beside the other pile. Grip the pile at your left with your left hand. Grip the pile at your right with your right hand. Be sure your thumbs face in! Take both piles with your thumbs and flip the cards up. Both piles will mix together and you will "shuffle" the cards. Push the piles together, so there is again only one pile. This is called **riffle-shuffle.**

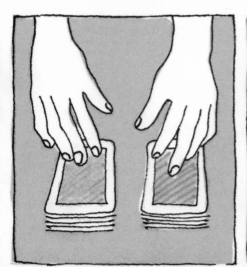 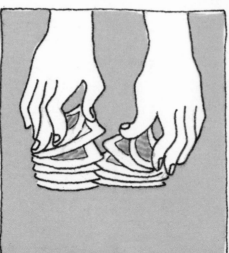 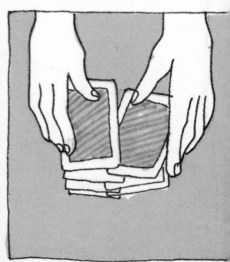

 **ONE ON ONE**

How to Do It

    1. Spread the cards face up on the table. Remove a jack and a 7 from the deck.

    2. Place these two cards face up next to each other on the table. Ask a friend to try to move the 7 under the jack without touching the jack. No one will be able to do this unless they know the secret!

 **The Secret**

Move the 7 *under* the table below the place where the jack is located.

GET TO KNOW THE DECK!
There are 52 cards in a deck, made up of 4 suits of 13 cards each. Two suits are black: spades ♠ and clubs ♣ .

Two suits are red: hearts ♥ and diamonds ♦ .

THE UPSIDE-DOWN PYRAMID

How to Do It

1. Take any ten cards from the deck. Place these cards as shown below. This shape is called a pyramid.

2. Ask your friends to try to make a new pyramid that points down instead of up. Tell them they must move only *three* of the cards to do this.

3 The Secret

Move Card G next to Card B. Then move Card J next to Card C. Place Card A in the middle, below Cards H and I. If you move only these three cards, you will get a pyramid that points down instead of up.

ANOTHER WAY TO SHUFFLE CARDS!

Put the pack of cards in one hand. With your other hand, pick up some of the cards from the bottom half of the deck. Slide these between the other cards and make one new pile. You can do this as many times as you like to make sure the cards are mixed well. This kind of shuffle is called **hand-over-hand.**

 **BOTTOMS UP!**

How to Do It

1. Look at the bottom card in the deck. Don't let anyone see you do this! Remember what the card is, but keep it a secret. Then put the deck of cards face down on the table.

2. Tell a friend to take any card from the deck without showing you the card.

3. Ask your friend to remember the card and then put it face down on top of the deck.

4. Now ask your friend to cut the cards. Then ask him or her to cut them again.

5. Now look through the deck to find your friend's secret card.

4 The Secret

You will find the secret card to the *right* of the card you remembered. It gets into this place the first time you cut the cards. The second cut does not change the order of those cards in the deck.

CUTTING THE CARDS

Don't use scissors! Place the deck of cards on the table. Take about half the cards from the top of the deck and put them in front of the bottom half. Then put the bottom half on top of the first half. The deck will be complete again.

THE ALMOST PERFECT CARD TRICK
How to Do It

1. Mix the cards.

2. Ask a friend to name the values of any three cards. For example: 5, 9, jack.

3. Tell your friend that you can make any two of the three named cards appear together in the deck.

4. Place the deck behind your back.

5. Now bring the cards in front of you. Then deal the cards one at a time on the table. Stop dealing as soon as two of the three cards appear together.

5 This trick is called the Almost Perfect Card Trick because, by chance, it works nearly all the time.

TIPS ABOUT CARDS

Dealing. Taking cards, one at a time, from the top of the deck and placing them face down on the table.

Face Down. Placing the cards so that their number or value *cannot* be seen.

Face Up. Placing the cards so you can see their numbers or values.

FIFTY-TWO PICKUP

How to Do It

   1. Put all 52 cards face up on the table.

   2. Leave your friends and go into a nearby room. From there, tell your friends that you want one of them to pick a card. Then he or she should show it to everyone and rub the card on the table. Then have that person mix it back in with the other cards.

   3. Return to the room and look at the cards on the table. Ask your friends if the card was a heart, a diamond, a spade, or a club.

   4. Look through the mixed-up cards and find the "secret" one. Hold it up for everyone to see.

The Secret

You will need a secret partner to help you with this trick. This person will secretly tap your foot to let you know what the card is: one tap for an ace, two taps for a 2, and so on. Have your partner tap you eleven times for a jack, twelve times for a queen, and thirteen times for a king.

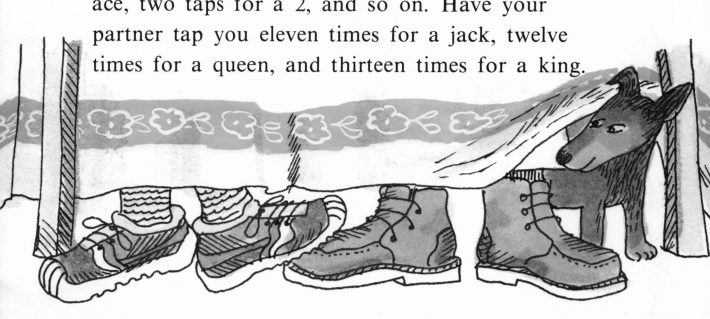

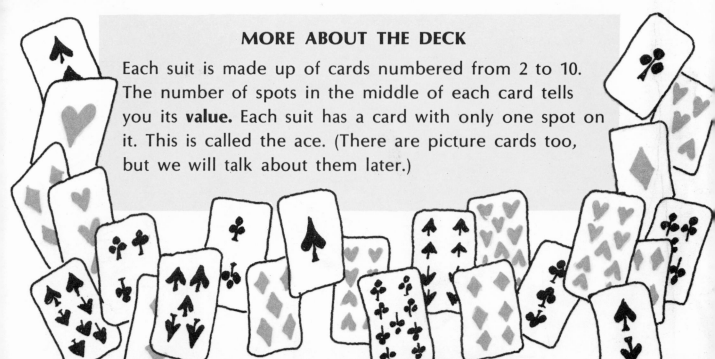

MORE ABOUT THE DECK

Each suit is made up of cards numbered from 2 to 10. The number of spots in the middle of each card tells you its **value.** Each suit has a card with only one spot on it. This is called the ace. (There are picture cards too, but we will talk about them later.)

7 THE FOUR MUSKETEERS

How to Do It

Before you begin, secretly find the four jacks and place them on top of the deck.

1. While your friends watch, deal the jacks face down side by side.

2. Give the rest of the deck to a friend.

3. Tell him or her to deal face down any number of cards. These should be placed on each of the four piles. Do this until there are no more cards.

4. Now tell your friend to look at the top card of each pile and remember them. He or she must keep the cards a secret.

5. Gather the cards. Place any pile on top of any other pile.

6. Tell your friend to cut the cards.

7. Deal all the cards face up, one at a time. You will be able to pick out the four hidden cards.

♣ 7 **The Secret**

A hidden card will come *after* every jack.

STILL MORE ABOUT THE DECK

There are three kinds of **picture**, or **face**, cards: the jack (or knave), the queen, and the king. The jack is the same as an 11, the queen the same as a 12, and the king is a 13.

 **CARD PALM READING**

How to Do It

1. Put any three cards face up on the table. Below is an example.

Give the rest of the cards to a friend who will secretly help you do this trick.

2. Ask another person to put his or her palm on the face of one of these cards while your back is turned. Wait a minute and then turn around.

3. Look carefully at each of the three cards. Then ask to see the palms of all the people in the room.

4. Point out the secret card and hold it up for everyone to see.

The Secret

The friend who is holding the rest of the cards is your helper. He or she uses thumb positions to "tell" you which card was touched.

Thumb like this means Card A is the one.

Thumb like this means Card B is the one.

Thumb like this means Card C is the one.

 **THE TOP-CARD TRICK**

How to Do It

1. Look at the bottom card in the deck. Don't let anyone see you, though! Remember what the card is, but keep it a secret.

2. Cut the cards. Keep the bottom half for yourself.

3. Ask your friend to look at the top card of his or her pile and to say out loud what it is. Look at the top card of your own pile and also "tell" what that card is.

4. Place your pile on top of your friend's pile. Cut the deck. Then the deck will be in one pile again.

5. Tell your friend that by snapping your fingers you can make both your cards come together in the deck.

6. Snap your fingers and search the deck. You will find both cards together!

The Secret

You only *pretend* to call out the card at the top of your pile. Instead, call out the bottom card you first saw.

DO YOU KNOW THAT...

Most new decks of cards have two extra cards, called **jokers.** These are not part of a suit. If you lose a card, you can use a joker to take the place of the lost card.

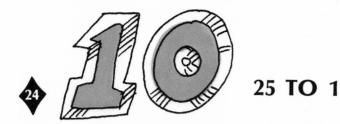
25 TO 1

How to Do It

1. Take 25 cards from the deck. Lay them out five rows across and five rows down.

2. Be sure to put them in this order, face up.

3. Ask a friend to look at any card and remember it. Then ask him or her to point to the row where the secret card is.

4. Gather up the cards row by row. You may place any row on top of any other. You should pick up the row that has the secret card *last*.

5. Deal the cards again exactly as you did before.

6. Again ask your friend to point to the row where the secret card is now.

7. Gather up the cards and then pull the secret card out of the deck.

10 The Secret

Your friend's secret card will be the one at the top of the row that he or she *last* pointed to.

FOOLING YOUR AUDIENCE

Your card tricks will look more exciting and secret if you add touches that may not have anything to do with the trick.

Put the deck of cards behind your back. It may not mean anything to the trick, but everyone who is watching you will think it does!

Snap your fingers. Again, it doesn't make the trick work or not work, but everyone will think it does.

THE ABOUT-FACE CARD

How to Do It

1. Spread the cards face down on the table. Ask a friend to take any card in the deck. Your friend should look at it without showing it to you.

2. Gather the rest of the cards together. Tell your friend to return the card face down to the top of the deck.

3. Take the deck in your hands behind your back. Now secretly turn the top, chosen card face up.

4. Show the bottom card of the deck to your friend while holding up the complete deck. Ask your friend if this is the correct card. Although you know it is not, this will give you a chance to see the secret card.

5. Place the deck behind your back again. This time turn the secret card back around so it faces down.

6. Place the deck face down on the table. Ask your friend to mix up the cards.

7. Look through the deck and find the secret card. Then hold it up for everyone to see.

11 The Secret

You show this card:

You *see* this card:

MORE TIPS FOR CARD TRICKS

Make your audience relax. It is easier to entertain people when they are comfortable. Tell them a tall tale. Tell them a funny joke. They will enjoy your tricks more if they are happy.

ORDER AND DISORDER

How to Do It

1. Take ten cards of the same suit, from ace to 10, from the deck.

2. Put these cards face down in order. The ace goes on top and the 10 should be on the bottom.

3. Tell a friend that you will lay these cards on the table any way he or she chooses. Your friend can tell you to "deal" or "duck" the card next in turn.

> **To deal** means to place the top card on the table face down.
>
> **To duck** means to place the top card under the *next* top card you are holding.

Then place both of these cards face down together.

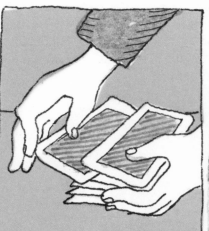

4. Tell your friend that by snapping your fingers you can make the cards appear in the order they were in at first.

5. Snap your fingers. Deal the cards face up on the table and they will appear as you said they would.

12 When you follow the directions exactly, you will see this trick works all by itself.

MORE TIPS ABOUT CARD TRICKS

Never tell the secret of how you do a card trick. If you do, your trick will no longer be a secret. Never show off all your tricks at the same time. Always save a few tricks for the next time!